Soon Every House Will Have One

Holly Hopkins

smith|doorstop

Published 2014 by
smith|doorstop Books
The Poetry Business
Bank Street Arts
32–40 Bank Street
Sheffield S1 2DS

ISBN 978-1-902382-09-8
Typeset by Utter
Printed by People for Print, Sheffield

Acknowledgements

Thanks go to the editors of the magazines in which some of
these poems first appeared: *Magma*, *The North*, *The Poetry
Review*, *The Rialto*, *The TLS* and *Verse Kraken* and also to the
editors of the anthologies: *Birdbook 1: Towns, Parks Gardens
& Woodlands*, *Bedford Square 7*, *Dear World and Everyone In
It: New Poetry in the UK* and *CAST: The Poetry Business Book
of New Contemporary Poets*.

smith|doorstop Books are a member of Inpress:
www.inpressbooks.co.uk. Distributed by Central Books Ltd.,
99 Wallis Road, London E9 5LN

The Poetry Business is an Arts Council
National Portfolio Organisation

Supported by
**ARTS COUNCIL
ENGLAND**

Contents

i.m. Beth Owen

Offchurch

The wheat is ready for cropping, a full congregation
beside the road through the fields from nowhere to dismantled nowhere,
a brick bridge over a thirsty ditch and the cedar holding up its green tray
are the only telltales that there was once a big house that went on fire
or was sold in parts like a butchered cow and sometimes,
one evening in five, a car will crawl through to a corrugated farm.

And this is the only time you took the walk with me,
and because you were there and could charm a fish out of its pond
and make it want to stand on its tail to please you,
a saucer-faced barn owl pushed out from the stag oak,
boated into the blue for a moment, then dropped down into the corn.

The King's Manor Cat

Someone sent you a vase with a bulbed base
round and weighty as a cantaloupe.
It smashed in the sorting office,
the fragments moved inside the envelope
so easily, the postman forced it
through your letter box: the wreckage
sliding like tectonic plates.

This is how we are born,
our skulls knit in our teens.
The grotesque movement enables safe delivery.

The problem is we risk sealing up completely.
The ossification continues like the famous cat
fed liver every elderly day until the vitamin A
fused it into one chalky block.

We must raise up the banners each morning
with the pulling back of the bedlinen.
We must not eat the liver.

Duck

You teach children how to give.
They tear bread into damp-fingered lumps
for you to shovel up in your snorkelling gear.

What excellent thrift
to make your feet from old umbrellas
and to colour yourself with muesli;

to eat the river's beard
where it sprouts between the cold washed scales
and to clean your own pond as you swim,
trailing a black ribbon through the glazed weed.

But though you can drag yourself up
and pass through the sky like a windscreen wiper,
and your voice is loud enough to fill in the river,
you cannot stop the treading.

The banks grow lush with shame
as they stamp out the fire on your tail.

Telephone Girls

Girls have always been joined to telephone systems.
Not just teenage gossips or nineteen-forties girls
in whale-fat lipstick, scalps smelling
of chemical burns for days after each perm,
girls plugged into circuit boards, primed for scandal,
heavy bakelite ear cones and mouthpieces rising
like snakes' heads up from their breasts;
that's not what I mean.
I mean anchorites – telephones to God.

They chose to be built into church walls:
Dame Julian of Norwich,
Emma of All Saints, North Street, York;
the masonry rising like a slow upward guillotine.
The simple engineers would leave a slot
to admit a parcel of light and air,
food and requested prayers.

They believed that in this pure removal they'd become
a prayer machine, that would bypass the pleading din.
That each day of their silence would be another stitch
sewing their lips and ears into the robes of God,
until their tears would fall directly in his lap.

Investing in Mannequins

I boxed them in a garage, unhooked limbs
from their hidden metal joints,
shrouded arms and legs in bubble wrap.

My boss bought from China, to eBay on
to small shops, army museums and men
who want light-weight life-sized women.

I did a photo-shoot in the living room,
on a carpet perfect as water tension.
Rigged each frozen girl in a cocktail dress
used double-sided tape to make the necklines
cling between hard, hollow breasts.
I wrote listings: *Debbie is a classy brunette ...*

The most I ever got was for a baby
with a bashed in hand. I started cheap,
called it *poor thing, needs a loving home*,
named her Lucy, took a picture of the hand
snapped off, empty as a chocolate bunny.

The bidders kept asking more questions
until I'd written a hometown, a date of birth,
a rainy motorway accident which killed both parents,
she went for three times the usual price.

International Women's Day

The tip of the stem's cut flat,
dry as the end of a pencil,
petals the pink of document wallets,
square, no longer in bud,
the type that will brown
before it yawns wide open.
Handed to me by a blonde ponytail
striding across the road
and for a moment I thought
I was an object of spontaneous pity,
until I remembered a dry concrete campus
outside Chengdu, where students
once gave me a corporate red rose
to celebrate this day, and now
the tradition's brought to London,
but this rose is flagging. Its leaves flop
despite the air saturated with drizzle
and I can't warm my hands
because I'm holding a rose.
I think about cutting a route
past parliament so I can get rid of it
at Pankhurst's black bronze feet,
or taking it home and waiting
for my boyfriend to ask who it's from.
The rain is starting to pick up
and the Garden Museum does cheap tea,
but perhaps they'll think I've stolen it.
A plastic banner on the railings
says: *Potato Day – Here Sunday*.

Margaret and her Cottage, Ontario

You're swimming across the lake on steel hips
your basalt bones are quite worn down
but with your new motor you're kicking to the island,
keeping your head up and dry, facing down the floating birds.

Behind you the boathouse is stark
its bright pine hasn't yet settled into the landscape.
Last year you had the outhouse re-dug, a two-seater
so it'd last longer. You won't need to do it again.
You're weighing up whether the jetty will need work
or if, rot-nibbled, it may last you.

And now you're holding your head out of water
not because you don't know the dip and glide of a good stroke
but for safety's sake, so the sudden motor boats
which ferry up weekenders and supplies
will see you, here where they don't expect you,
so far out from the land.

Bicycle Woman

In the immediate aftermath of the accident
they couldn't get me to hospital
and all the surgeon had was the bicycle
he'd been Sunday riding at the time

so that is why my lungs inflate and deflate
with this bicycle pump
and why I have to run this pedal
with my left hand to keep my heart going.

You understand I am grateful,
but sometimes my back being lashed
to this trapezoid frame makes it swell
with fire. And I miss the way my skin

was warm and seemed to glow
before the grafts with rubber.
The doctors have prescribed black oil
that I must rub into my spine each night

and if I shut my teeth too quick
there's the ding of a bell.
It's a clear sound, shunts me awake
when I'm desperate for a blanket sleep

and not another night of free-wheeling
down country roads in a chute of high hedges
or of pad-locking my ankles together
and lying on my side against a lamppost.

Explanation for those who don't know love

I have a child and am more important
than childless people.

I am two people and have an extra vote.
You cannot comprehend our bond,

it is mysterious and I am greater because of it,
so in a tie-break situation I am three people.

My daughter is five and very bright for her age,
this requires special consideration.

She is a delight and centres every conversation
like a fantastic table decoration.

If she breaks your possessions
it's an interrogation of their meaning,

a state of blissful questioning that you have lost.
If she cries it's only because she wants something,

she can't yet comprehend the magnitude of grief
so it is not selfish like when you cry.

The Flayings

A detergent-cup of glue in a flat-roofed primary school;
fingers dip, find dry PVA peels off in strips,
membranes holding a crazed pattern of skin.
Or it can be rubbed off, dropping smuts
like those left when rubbing out mistakes. It escalates,

to a childhood fascination with flame
the slow seduction of wax, tipping the candle
to encourage long lines to slip down, to puddle.
A knuckle picks up a small white helmet
which can be removed when set. This hurts,

now we're ready for skin. A flash-roast summer,
strappy tops and our flesh scarlet by tea time.
When we wash off the day our skin comes away
in white webbing leaving nibbled coastlines,
red islands. We burn that night in our beds.

You'd think that would prepare us
for the day we stand in a lift and see ourselves
in the back mirror, the canned light bloating us
like drowned things. This soft pudge, our inventory.
No more waiting to split out of a shell.

Stratigraphy

It's hard to be an archaeologist:
years of study, competition, applications
so you can kneel all day, in the ground,
tugging the soil back one blanket at a time.

It's a discipline that destroys the evidence as it goes.
Rates of sunburn and alcoholism are high;
and a trowel lasts at best a year
before the blade's worn away
in a fleshless demonstration of what happens to the hand.

Time doesn't always do its job.
I knew a guy: gave up digging
after clearing a churchyard in Kent.
A lead-lined coffin is better than Tupperware,
and the child's face was perfect as a new bar of soap.

I Have Chosen to Become a Plasterer

I want to smooth the world under light but firmly held tools.
I have practised by cutting bread without pressure on the knife:
just the brisk back and forth, allowing the thinnest slice
to curl away from the loaf like a fleece-flap lolling back
as the farmer draws across his electrical shears.

My boyfriend says I am sure to be a success.
He says middle-classes love employing middle-classes,
that's why his parents got Bill the sculptor
to make their kitchen cupboard doors.

Starlings

We'd heard the fens were dying seas
pinned into their beds by reeds;
the sedges crowded out our path
through the washed-out winter marsh.

They came in ragged lines that fell
into the budding chirping swell
of bodies caught up in a flow
that stretched itself like kneaded dough

until the churning shoal was black
and hemmed within a living sack
that smashed itself across the dusk
but could not break the thread of trust

that held each bird beside another,
and pulled the molten flock together
until they turned and plunging down
were hooked into the weedy ground.

We both stood locked inside our coats
and in the dark we neither spoke
in case our clumsy blundering
upset the other's newfound wings.

England, where did you go?

England of the burrow-in green, the chalk galvanised giant,
undulating earth-bank fortress, the flinted Roman wall,
the full flair gorse, messy hay-trails waiting
to be bin-bag-baled by steel mandibles:

you unroll through the window of a train,
but should I get out in search of you, you'd be off,
and I'd be left wandering down dual carriageways,
looking across bean fields and filthy ditches.

Country Churches

They slip their moorings in the night,
glide down tarmac roads
to a city where evangelicals
are taking over bingo halls, old cinemas,
calling, singing, hot in electric light.

The Gesture

Your speech is written on this nub of paper:
one of those large tissue sheets shop assistants use
to wrap wine bottles or china lamps,
we have compressed it to an inch block.
As you speak, unfold it carefully or it will tear,
unfold it prudently to get it in the right order.

The camera is looking to slice you.
We have drawn the allowed shape
behind you on the wall.
Anything that goes over
will be cut off: fingers
or elbows sawn through the bone.

We need names for the way
he shakes out his wrists,
for his cage of fleshy fingers.

Freeze frame on the audience.

Now, zoom in on a face,
take an acetate sheet
and trace the features.

Repeat.

Layer them up
like a plastic phone book.

Voila:
you have mapped the average
reaction
where the ink is darkest.

Antonio, Duke of Milan

I was the one who met with generals
negotiated pay and bonuses
to keep the city safe from our own men.

Everyday he made less effort
and bought more books.

Not that there weren't good ones,
An Atlas of the Indies, six feet long,
large enough to sit around at dinner.

Or a book of hours, size of an apricot,
more gold leaf than letters.
It took a monk sixteen years
on an island in the Northern sea
working each day except
when winter froze his ink.

But most had covers sagging off,
brown leper's skin,
yet he had them carried
through the city under escort
like statues of the Virgin during festivals.

I said, 'You need to think about your people.'
But it was like he'd eaten all that dust.
His wife died and he didn't even notice.

Malcontents started to print pamphlets.
The Duke as a necromancer in long robes
talking to the devil, lying with harlots.
I showed mercy, split a few nostrils,
cut off ears, but the damage was done.

By then he was mad.
He wanted a library,
a hall of books anyone could use.
We'd have the Papal armies on us in a month.

I said we couldn't afford it,
anyway we've printing presses now;
books are getting cheaper
soon every house will have one.

But he said books were only half the point,
that people needed space to think:
went on about shared rooms where the baby's crying
and there's shouting through the walls.

                              As if those people read!

So I gave him space.

Put him on a boat and shipped him off,
although I let him have his wailing brat,
let him keep her dressed in white lace now.

The City Cut from a Mountain

We waited for the windiest day to burn the forest,
flame handed from branch to waving branch.
High-pressure hoses cleared the soil,
the loose shale, until it was naked as an egg.

Then lasers, drills, giant crunching worms,
sand-blasters, down and in:
it made a ringed city, with a spiral road
that opened gently as a paper flower in water.

The houses were for us, winners of a lottery.
We left the broken glass of the old city,
that bowl of smog between chalk hills,
to live inside high granite walls.

In summer the rock was cool.
In winter, water from hot springs
was forced through drilled capillaries
until our houses shone with warmth.

That first New Year's we built bonfires
on our roofs, cooked sausages on sticks,
wore our city uniforms of white wool.
Everything was fixed. Everyone fitted.

If you had two kids you had two bedrooms.
Later, if you had two bedrooms you had two kids.
In some studio flats, they found children
carved from the rock, polished red stone.

Gaining Height in the City

We try to get up high so we can see where we're going,
but buildings bank the street like police in riot gear
and even vans are bigger than the rooms we live in.

Winter is the worst; the trees have lost their illusions.
They're scaly bone and do not hide
the concrete rising behind them.

When we lived in a cathedral city, we walked round
and round the medieval walls like a dog
chained to a stake. Now we've moved to the capital

the only space is the sweep of the river.
Here the sun grins in the windows on the opposite bank
and for a moment we think we the have space to choose.

The gulls show us the current. They pull
themselves out of the black water and fly upstream
landing in a white skid only to drag past us again.

The Future

You were so thin you'd slip into any future you chose.
You'd walk up to strangers
and find out the names of their children.

Do you still wear loose dresses from thrift stores
which only a paper knife could wear?
Do you still cut your own hair?

When you fly back to visit us
will you still find chimney pots cute
and love the English habit of geraniums?

I can't imagine you walking through metal detectors
at a school with your mug in the staffroom.
I can't imagine you tired on Friday afternoons.

You're always in the rooms we painted yellow.
It's a summer evening after our finals
and we wait, puffed overgrown cuckoos.

Anglepoise

It throws a yellow net and waits
with cool bones, hot head and aching elbow –
patient as the man who stands, arm out,
holding bottle after bottle
for marathon runners to grab at as they pass.

It condemns me, says:
Your head is empty as an eggshell scraped clean
waiting to be turned over and have its bottom bashed in.
No matter how hard you work
you can only glean the smallest sliver of all that is,
tiny as the filament in my empty bulb. See how it glows.